AF557840

A Mirror unto Ourselves

BY THE SAME AUTHOR

In Your Face

Get to the Top

Mantras for Success

A Mirror unto Ourselves

Suhel Seth

HAR-ANAND
PUBLICATIONS PVT LTD

Views and facts presented in the book are those of the author and the publishers are not responsible for the same.

Published by Ashok Gosain and Ashish Gosain for:
HAR-ANAND PUBLICATIONS PVT LTD
E-49/3, Okhla Industrial Area, Phase-II, New Delhi-110020
Tel: 41603490
E-mail: info@haranandbooks.com/haranand@rediffmail.com
Shop online at: www.haranandbooks.com

Printed in India at Aarya Printers.

Preface

Books which are a collection of columns seem to suggest author laziness but not in this case. For me, they are not only reminiscent of the past and the affairs in the tides of men but equally suggestive of the evolution of us as people; society or nation. To that end, they are effective chroniclers as well.

My first book which was a collection of columns was published in 2002 and titled *In your Face*: this one is *A Mirror unto Ourselves*: there's a reason for not calling this in typical sequel manner, *In your Face,* 2. Much has changed in this fine country of ours: some for the good and some for the bad. India today is a throbbing nation where a lot of stigmas have been swept aside by technology and societal evolution. The young are no longer seeking marquee jobs nor are they stifled by peer pressure to do what is the "right" thing. Empowerment is not a hand-me-down any longer. We have moved from being ultra-conservative to being truly liberal, at least in some quarters. We have a young population that is willing to ask questions of those who govern us without the attendant fear that existed a decade ago. Social media has given people wings: some leading to flights of fancy and others to flights of destruction but that is how it is.

We are seeing greater accountability across the board and in almost everything we do or touch which to my mind, is a good thing. We no longer have any holy cows except the holy cow if you know what I mean? We are also faced with a situation where people are being judged without being truly tested. But that's par for the course. Anonymity on social media has made people both brave and reckless and the time is not far when there will be a mechanism to separate the wheat from the chaff but till then, there will be turmoil as there often is when societies and people within not only grapple with new technologies but equally with new ideas. Many would argue this is the age of disruption. But for many this is also the age of anger and the age of cocooning oneself.

The columns that have been selected for this book do not have a theme because life does not have one single theme. These are columns which reflect on the kind of people we are and what we have become. The columns may, to the reader, seem judgmental but they were never written with a clear idea of what's right and what's wrong: that is for reader interpretation as it should be. Nor these literary works in the classic sense since the environment in which they were first published was newspapers which are current and not necessarily meant as classics in the traditional sense.

I have believed that when one writes, one should write with a sense of fearlessness but equally with a sense of purpose. Being apolitical; secular and with no agenda in mind has helped me raise issues which have, and continue to, resonate with people. We may have new Governments and new rulers in place but at times we live with old ailments. It almost feels like history being re-visited in the present and at times the present seems dangerously like the past but then that is the reality of the times we live in.

I hope you find these columns interesting: and I choose the word 'interesting' carefully: all form of writing be it in print or on digital media must invent curiosity. It must stoke the mind and then allow for the mind to take a final call. Interesting also because for many, there will be personal experiences and tales that they can warm up to in these columns. Because they are not about a make-believe world but instead reflections on the world we inhabit today.

In many ways, it is a mirror and like every mirror, deception goes with the territory: mirrors delight as much as they disgust. For me personally, these columns truly are a mirror unto ourselves whether we like it or not. I hope you concur as you go through the pages of this book.

SUHEL SETH

3 December 2018

Contents

I

Oh, Kolkata!

After several years, I spent six nights in Kolkata, which, thankfully enough, were like spending six nights in heaven after the kind of lives we lead in the Delhis and Mumbais of the world. There are no pressures of work; there is almost an embedded fait accompli in people's demeanour, which many a time suggests that this is the pace we follow, and bad luck to you if you don't like it. I also had the luxury of spending these six nights in unbridled comfort at what is certainly the finest resort hotel in India: the ITC Sonar Bangla. The editor of this paper, M.J. Akbar, thankfully agrees that the charm of Kolkata has still not dimmed, which is why the last time he and I were in Kolkata together we spoiled ourselves at the various impromptu dinners that were held in our honour.

There is also a certain basket of values that never escapes Kolkata. The city just doesn't care who you are as long as you, at some time in your life, have been a part of it. Which is why even the empty bars tools at the Light Horse Bar at Saturday Club tell you tales you may have heard aeons ago. The butter chicken at Kwality's tastes just as good and thank god the ever evolving Priya Paul has done nothing to modernise the cuisine of Flury's which still serves up the best rum cakes and chicken patties! I went back to some of our theatre haunts and remembered with great affection the time I spent with Ashoke Viswanathan savouring the Afghani chicken at Sutripti or partaking of Bacchus' generosity at Chota Barrister.

I even drove past the famed Lover's Lane several times just to relive those moments when we would sneak our girlfriend of the time to play hooky under a starry sky until the ubiquitous Kolkata sergeant would show up on his well-preserved Bullet motorcycle. I watched with fondness the various cricket matches going on in the Maidan and the same Maya Ram paobhaji being advertised with gusto. I took an afternoon off and strolled within the corridors of Jadavpur University and was delighted to see Tommy Hilfiger stickers outside the SFI office: even the communists have realised the worth of Tommy.

But has Kolkata really changed? Have the people become smarter in terms of making the best of every opportunity? I think not. And this is why Kolkata is still such a special place to be. The only place where a lunch is incomplete without a Campari; where there is a distinction between the dining room and the smoking room and where round-collared T-shirts still find no acceptance in club bars. There is also a certain panache that Kolkata has with regard to the music you hear. Item girls and Daler Mehndi have still not replaced Barry Manilow or for that matter Nat King Cole. There are hundreds who can still recite their school song and have preserved their college blazers and not replaced them with some foreign brands. Where photographs are in photo frames and not in cupboards, so that you can litter your drawing room with garish vases. It is this about the city that makes it so special.

I took long walks in the malls only to witness for myself, first-hand,the consumerism that has invaded Kolkata and then I thought to myself, why not. If Kolkata can erect malls and frequent them without forgetting the Victoria Memorial or the National Library, then more power to its collective elbows. I smiled when I saw the queue of people trying to enter the American Centre. In no other city are libraries as crowded as cinema halls. And that is because Kolkata still has a mind when all others are busy losing theirs.

Many years ago I was part of a movement called "Concern for Calcutta" and it delighted me no end to see that Ward 63 was still sprinkled with the work that CC, as it was known then, was doing. It is perhaps the only city in the world which has a nature study park in the costliest real estate of that city. I went to Dalhousie Institute and saw an impromptu quiz just as I went to CC&FC and saw prompted drinking happening. The other unique dimension about this city is, if you belong here, you are never a guest when you return.

The family asks you no questions: it merely expresses unbridled delight in seeing you back. You can walk into dinners and parties alike; to cricket matches and merchant's cup soccer matches on the back of your past. Kolkata doesn't really care about the present or what you are upto!

The visit was even more special because I staged two shows of our English play Alipha: and the memories rushed back of a time when I would be staging a play almost once every three months. The halls as beautiful and the audience as well-behaved. No one picking up his or her mobile phone and screaming Advani or Sonia. Just watching what they've come to watch intently and with the respect it deserves.

Sometimes, only sometimes, I wish we could throw the residents out of Delhi and replace them with Kolkatans. The purging would mean so much to all of us. But then when one ponders, one is gratified that Kolkata is still a city of remarkable joy.

Of prose and passion.

Of poetry and phuchka.

Of people and, thankfully, no prejudices.

2

Are We in Dior Straits

Take a look at the women jostling to get into Jacques Dessage in Delhi or for that matter into that silly luxury mall built on illegal forest land in Delhi and one would never imagine there is a recession. By the same token, look at some of those little darlings in Bombay who are getting manicured and pedicured for the IPL only so that they can look better than Dhoni, and once again you wouldn't imagine any meltdown except for some of their fat at some ultra-chic spa in Baden-Baden. So is there really a recession? Are we living in troubled times? Or is the recession only for the poor or the really very rich? Or are some of the scoundrel husbands just fabricating all of this so that the wives spend less than what they used to which in other words means a Birkin a fortnight and not one every week!

I am a great believer that women in India are recession-proof. At least some of them certainly are. I cannot ever imagine Parmeshwar Godrej wearing the same beret to a party unless of course she is shooting for a documentary on AIDS and needs it for continuity. I cannot for the life of me think of a day when we will have women shying away from the lure of an LV bag or for that matter a Dior dress or even to taste truffles when all their lives they have only been exposed to khaandvi but then such is life and such are the vagaries of high living. Do you ever think that my dear friend Queenie Dhody will give up wearing the finest of the best or for that matter will Shahnaaz Hussain lower the height of her bouffant in solidarity with the falling sensex? Likewise, it will be a long time before many of the quick-rich real estate wives in Delhi actually stop their weekly botox injections and actually start looking like God wishes them to. The little that I know about this high-society lot is that recession is something that they discuss kike you would malaria. You feel sad but you let it known that you haven't got it. Which brings to me yet another interesting point: the most discussed thing among these rich women is actually the recession though Chidambaram would still like us to call it a slow-down. Be whatever the hell it is, the fact is that the rich aren't becoming poor in this country of ours in a hurry. Look at their homes? Look at the number of fashion weeks that India is going to suffer? I am slowly coming to the opinion that India will slowly get to the point where we will have as many fashion weeks as fashion designers: which means every week we are going to have a show commemorating one miserable tailor or the other and then you can have the chuffed Chairman of a tobacco company feeling as good as politicians when they win elections.

We need these women to strike out in protest. We need them to live in a land where recession and job losses are alien concepts. We need them to spend and not save. They in many ways are re-defining the way the world must behave if it needs to slide back into consumerism and some order. These women are doing yeoman service to the financial health of the world and must be lauded. Seriously. They are the ones keeping that Parisian luggage maker alive. These are the women who keep Biki Oberoi in business so that he can command high rentals from stores that are hardly visited. These are the women who have shown exemplary courage of their conviction and their fatal belief in the financial muscle-power of their husbands. In many ways, these women represent strength, courage and fortitude.

Sundays were the days of rest. Sabbath as it were. But look around you, in these so-called tough times, and you will see these women in their resplendent best: Sundays are for those infamous brunches where terrible food must be washed down with complimentary champagne; when you actually take out the husband's convertible to let your hair down and show the world how well he really is doing even though he may be in prison because he defaulted on paying the Xerox-shop. But these are the realities of our times.

It is true that India is carrying on magnificently well. Even Gandhi's belongings were brought back by a man who has hardly ever walked except within his Maybach to change some silly CD perhaps. The irony of India is that our slums win Oscars and our fancy houses get written about even if they are in Kensington. Jai ho. And I could have said more post Jai Ho but then some silly political party has bought the rights to the song. Another sign that we are not in recession. If the ruling party can afford to pay for Jai Ho, then are we really living in tough times or just Dior straits?

(Suhel Seth is Managing Partner of Counselage and an irreverent observer of life: Suhel@counselage.com)

3

A Cleaner, Healthier, Possibly Greener India?

No matter what the cynics may say about development being opposed by poverty-stricken countries and the fact that basics need to get sorted out before we do the window-dressing, the last few years have been remarkable for India and what we have been able to achieve: sometimes by the shrillness of our activists; sometimes by the activism of our judiciary and at others by the will of the Government.

When Delhi had to adopt CNG there was a hue and cry and it finally happened: sure there was pain; there was very little planning and a lot of people suffered: there were queues of autos outside filling stations and so on but eventually the capital was gifted cleaner air cleaner skies. Sometimes initiatives like these have to be enforced since they run contrary to populism and at times I wish we took more such steps in the face of political opportunism but then again I guess that is asking for too much! I believe the enforcement of CNG by the venerable Supreme Court established one thing for sure: there are conditions that can be created where populism can and must be replaced wit realism; where the pleasures of today must be sacrificed for the rewards of tomorrow and each one of us is not the usurper but the custodian of the planet and all that it stands for, too that end, the whole CNG exercise was a watershed in re-defining India's eco-sensitivity.

More recently, we had witnessed utterances and mild protestations from Anbumani Ramadoss our Health Minister about the bad examples that celebrities were setting by smoking in public or in fact smoking at all. He then went on to create conditions for highly restrictive tobacco sale and then topped it up with enforcing a public ban from 2 October (chosen wisely in the name of the Mahatma) on all smoking in public places or covered areas. I always believed a ban was necessary. Passive smoking kills and it is this that I am against. Every smoker has a right to smoke himself to death but he does not have the right to be the vehicle of disease dissemination so that ban was not only critical but opportune as well. In the last two years almost all of the EU is smoke-free as far as public areas are concerned. Many hotels in Europe have stopped offering smoking rooms too and I believe the Taj Group in India has shown exemplary conduct by following this new law to the hilt.

I believe any law such as the one Ramadoss has established is only as good as its enforcement: but then again there are two kinds of pressures that will bear results: one where you ensure that the ban exists and establishments are made fiscally responsible and the other where you create an environment of social pressures. In America, social pressure and legal pressure have co-existed in the area of tobacco-control and this is the example that India will also have to graduate towards. We will need to build silos of awareness from the bottom up. I remember when I was advising the Delhi Government on pollution, we began the campaign with children as our primary target: the campaign to ban plastic and crackers was driven through children and the pressure they existed on adults including of course their own families. I believe the time has come for an integrated campaign, which not only uses fear but also positive values to create a culture of abstinence from tobacco; companies like ITC and GPI need to be targetted by Government through even more excessive taxation: look at what Michael Bloomberg has achieved with cigarette pack pricing in New York: but then this battle will be comprehensively won only if we include all forms of tobacco: cigarette companies are soft targets because they are institutionalized: people like manufacturers of gutka, pan Masala and bidis get away with blue murder: they too must receive the harshest of punishment if we actually want to see results which will endure.

There is no question that we need to eliminate cigarettes and other forms of tobacco from our world. But then that is asking for the moon. That will never happen. Not at least in the short term. What we do need to focus on is the eradication of the disease. This ban is a battle-winning proposition but not a war-winning step and this is what we will need to do if we are serious about the ban.

Media will have to lay its own role and will have to have the courage to take these cigarette companies on despite the advertising losses they may suffer. We have seen many courageous media attempts wilt at the altar of greed and avarice and for far too long the gutka manufacturer or the cigarette company has been able to manipulate thought by managing the media. This will need to change if we want a lasting impact.

The dice has been cast. The game has begun and the criticality is so extreme that no one can afford to lose this game. Ramadoss for all his sins must be complimented on his courage and stand even if it is either accidental or motivated. What we now need to do is spread the ban; curb the supply and eradicate the vehicle. That is the only way forward.

4

Air Traffic Confusion

Much has been said and written about the airline business in the last few weeks. Talks of a bailout where none has happened. Talks of the airlines' bosses arm-twisting the politicians and enough acrimony between the ministers themselves. If this is not enough cause for air traffic confusion, then what is? Add to this, the limited information that almost all segments have about this whole issue and you have a lethal concoction, which will not only endanger this segment but will also, create long-term business imperatives that will do more harm than good!

But the realities of what this will mean for the economy can hardly be wished away. We are seeing a warped taxation policy being pursued by the Government of India: this will only do two things: it will force the airlines to start route rationalization and this means all the non-lucrative routes will become even more expensive (amongst which will be the PM's vote-bank region of the North-East) as also basic pricing will go out of whack. Qantas began a 30% route cut as part of route rationalization in June this year since in today's times, it is cheaper to ground rather than fly an aircraft. When this rationalization occurs in India, you will see scarcity of product (airline seats) and skyrocketing prices just when belt-tightening will also be taking place thanks to the stellar performance of our stock market. So what will happen and what is it that we need to do?

There is no question that in today's scenario, the civil aviation business in India is not just an economic generator but equally, a large employer as well. There have been huge investments (some sound and some unintelligent) in this sector: both direct and indirect and privatization is no longer indexed to airlines themselves but to airports and allied services be it ground handling or catering or for that matter charter companies: some of them do perform a non-elitist role as well if one considers their contribution to opening up of some of India's high-value tourism destinations. Then there is the whole issue of infrastructure that this sector needs in creating airports; either through public-private partnership or as a stand-alone exercise. If we do not analyse the impact shrinking airlines, we will fail to estimate the collateral damage that will be caused to the peripheral businesses that are built around the airline business. You can't expect private companies to build airports, which will have no traffic!

In recent days, one facet that has escaped attention of the so-called hawks is the increase in fares of low cost carriers: a ticket between Delhi and Calcutta is now retailing at Rs 12,000: a four-fold increase: true, there are still the Rs 99 offers but they are scarce. Then you have some low cost carriers re-inventing themselves: GO is now offering business class services for the price of an economy ticket: but please note the fine-print: it is at economy fares and not the low cost ones that we had all become used to. The villains in this piece are many:

- states in India are levying a state sales tax of anywhere between 25% to 32% on ATF (aviation turbine fuel): but the catch is not just the obscenely high tax: the base rate of the ATF that is being offered by the oil companies is double the international price of fuel at today's rates: so while Murli Deora has every right to berate the airlines for not paying the oil companies on time, the truth of the matter is, they are not selling ATF: they are instead indulging in day-light robbery and the cartel is they, not the airlines
- the Airports Authority of India charges the highest for any aircraft related activity: for instance the landing charges in India are the highest anywhere in the world; add to that the infrastructure limitations in terms of runways and you have yet another dangerous situation; every minute you spend hovering in the air, costs a fortune at today's ATF rates: but yet again, this is not being factored in
- you then have an alarming situation of political interference in retrenchment issues: Naresh Goyal was silly to take back all those people: and I have the fullest sympathy for those who did lose their jobs: they had no business to be axed in the manner they were but that is no excuse for the manner in which they were welcomed back: everyone knows that the political class leaned on Naresh Goyal and he wilted: in the process, you have created a new spectre of demonic activity qua employees and the political class
- then there is the final issue of an alliance between Kingfisher and Jet: I believe this just had to happen and history will bear this as the right decision but what both airlines will have to watch for is not just the fact that this will be viewed as anti-trust or monopolistic but even from a

perspective of pricing, there will have to be demonstrable restraint: the airlines would be better off grounding their planes rather than causing greater anguish to the common man through increased fares: because then they will lose both consumer trust and public empathy to their cause: they are in the dog-house already as far as the politicians are concerned: they cannot afford to anger the average consumer too

Globally, the civil aviation is either being supported by sovereign initiatives or very favourable laws. If Chapter 11 were not there, half of America's aviation business would have vanished overnight. We are seeing global consolidation and even more alliances: the fact that British Airways and American Airlines are in talks is enough of an indication. This is the way forward across the globe so we in India can no longer wear blinkers and imagine we will be safe from these externalities. It is not enough to indulge in tokenism by increasing the credit period for payment of oil dues: you have to strike at the heart of it all: the problem is with policy and our inability to take vital but unpopular steps: akin to a take-off that is destined to crash!

(Suhel Seth is Managing Partner of Counselage and on the Global Advisory Board of British Airways)

5

Republic of Disasters

There is almost a level of indifference that seizes the country when it comes to either warning our own of disasters or even more, when it comes to both preparing for the disaster and its aftermath. What we are seeing in Bihar is no different from what we see when terrorism strikes. The Indian state is a hapless witness to death and destruction in a way signaling its callousness and disregard for human suffering. Is it because we have just too many people and don't really care if a few million become a footnote? Or is there something deeper in our psyche, which just prevents us from being more humane than we really are? I wonder if any NGO or media organisation has ever filed an application with the RTI on exactly what goes on with the Prime Minister's Relief Fund? How much money is collected and how much actually reaches the ones who are suffering?

Every disaster in India has a familiar plot: national leaders will race against time and each other to get on the first chopper for an aerial survey post which there are promises and more promises. Of succour either in the form of compensation or in terms of relief material. Then there is the role of our venerable media. The headlines will focus on the plight of the people: boats wading through flooded villages make for very good television but do we ever go beyond that? And how does every Indian contribute? Do we dip into our pockets and give generously to those who had very little in the first place and are now deprived of everything that you can even imagine? Or do we limit it to television talk shows and the cursory dining table talk so that we come across as humane and full of empathy?

The problem with our country I imagine is we just don't give a damn. It really doesn't matter or merit attention as long as it doesn't happen to us. And in the metros it may never happen. In some strange way, the cruel hand of God also only strikes those who can hardly defend themselves either from nature's fury or for that matter from the lethargy of Governments. It is they who actually suffer and ironically, it is they who are the bulwark of every election cry. The sad bit is that the politician will use this very base of people to come to power and never ever care about them. Bihar is not just a national tragedy. It is a national shame. A shame that we can't protect our own and when they need help, most of us would turn the other way. Even the mechanism of planning and distributing the relief is awry.

This is something that we in India need to change. All this talk of inclusive growth is meaningless when we cannot even save lives; when we cannot even guarantee basic livelihood standards to our people and what's more when we cannot even create a movement that will inspire caring and giving back. In all of the last three weeks I have not seen a single industry statement forming a movement, which will help Bihar, come back into its own. Is it not strange that the same Bihar contributes more IAS officers and doctors to this country?

There are some heroes who continue to work and they need to be applauded. But no, we won't have the magnanimity to do that either. It is the army that is the saviour every time tragedy strikes and yet we quibble about increasing their pay? There are websites like coolbihari.com, which are doing sterling work in terms of creating awareness and raising funds, and yet they will never find mention in national media only because they don't have star journalists or high-profile editors at the helm. So the mess continues happily until the next tragedy. What is worse, while we have a National Disaster Management policy, we have zero implementation!

What this nation needs to be alarmed about is we can't talk about growth and demographic dividend if we allow our countrymen to perish every time a natural disaster strikes. We can't focus on Singur and the Mamatas of this world, if we don't care about the children who will never have a future in this country? They should be the real focus of our energies. We can't talk about Brand India and gleaming factories if we also have barren lands and flooded fields with our very own clinging on for precious life. The dichotomy is punishing and must begin to hurt our conscience. That is if we have one left!

6

Of Words on Paper and Prayers on One's Lips...

When we were growing up in Calcutta, we were fed on a diet of literature, which was almost always heavily loaded in favour of poetry. To this day, Calcutta takes pride in the fact that not just a Nobel but even a Poet Laureate was born within its confines. I remember picking up Tagore's short stories to only be told that while Hungry Stones was a superb tale, the great man's poetry was infinitely better. And then the Nobel and the Gitanjali happened.

In school, our literary nest was filled with nuggets from a Harivansh Rai Bachchan and a Nirala on the one hand and Auden, Shelley and Keats on another. Wordsworth was my inspiration for the appreciation of flowers and I can still say with my heart on my hand, that I read about daffodils long before I saw them as also the tiger was burning brightly on paper before vanishing from our game parks.

Amongst all the literary forms that exist, there is nothing more personal than poetry and the danger with poetry is precisely this: it can be so personal that it may only remain a conversation between the poet and his pen. And because it is so truly personal, it allows for realms of expression which fiction may replicate but can rarely surpass. In the times of yore, while historians captured the travails of those times, the poets were the ones who captured the emotional essence of that cultural moment. They were the chroniclers of romance and war; they were the ones who were mirrors of the literary evolution that those times must have gone through and to that end, poets were perhaps the finest souls: they captured emotions and then presented them but these emotions were personal; they were interpretations and introspection, but very rarely commentaries as perhaps some of Shakespeare's political plays were.

Last week India threw up a very unusual poet, He began as a lawyer and then moved onto national politics. He drew from experiences as varied as being involved in romantic dalliances outside St Stephen's College to comments about the state of the Indian Democracy. But not all his poems are just a reflection of the various hues of his life. Where his book of poems 'I witness' scores is that some of the poems are comments in rhyme but comments that don't merely stay on paper; they are evocative and appeal to perhaps a latent thought that we may all have. When he talks of John the Muslim, the poem is reflective of the malaise that has set into our political system. The fact that communalism is now a political weapon and must be harnessed at will. More than the poems being reflective, they also tell a tale. A tale of perhaps missed opportunities; of perhaps destroying the edifice of secularism and unity that this country was built on.

But what is even more interesting is that while these poems are a rendering of the churning of mind and soul, the medium that they were captured on is a cell phone and therein lies the irony. The most personal thoughts of modern man known to the external world are poems and this poet used the most intrusive medium to capture them on. Almost wishing to give them a voice.

I went through the entire book over one evening. An evening, which made me, travel in the Nano and took me to Oxford Street. An evening, which made me, connect with the chaatwala and the chowkidar. An evening where I could reflect on betrayal and trust and then see the anguish of falling standards in our judiciary. It was an enchanting evening.

Only because Kapil Sibal has been a superb witness. And an outstanding chronicler!

From lawyer to politician to poet. Sibal has now arrived full circle. It is a reflection of the times that we live in, that there are such few poets and even fewer people with a prayer on their lips. Kapil took me back in time to Calcutta. Where rhyme and verse were the touchstones of mental evolution. To that end, this book does a tremendous service: to the mind and the heart.

7

The Politics of Opportunism

I always gave great credit to the Communists for their ability to comprehend the maze of realpolitik in India which is why I am pretty surprised that they have been unable to fathom the ways of the Samajwadi Party and Amar Singh's new-found love for a Congress dining table. The truth of the matter is that in today's India, no political party has any ideology: all they have is a keen determination to hang onto the vestiges of power and all that comes with it.

I see no possible threat to this Government and not because they have dithered over every possible issue but only because there are no real issues that they can fight the next elections over. The manner in which our economy is in a downward spiral doesn't seem to bother anyone either. The fact is we as a nation are reeling. Never ever have we faced the kind of slowdown that has emerged and all this talk of inflation vanishing in three months is just that: talk. When we boast of being an economic superpower, we also have to come to terms with the realities of being indexed to global economies: these are different times from the ones we witnessed when the dragon economies collapsed. Today, whether it is our services businesses (which are 55% of our GDP) or the declining trends of agriculture, we cannot but escape the realities of being part of a global order. That global order itself is collapsing around us.

I have always maintained that while our Governments know how to be in power they can rarely govern and the fact that the so-called dream team is today faltering is no aberration: it is what exists. The farmer loan waiver has, to my mind, seriously undermined our banking system and we are quite willing to let that pass only because no political party can even afford to object to it. One more sign of opportunism, at the cost of national interest. The fact that in India today, we are comfortable with crippling our aviation sector because of rogue taxes is again reflective of how myopic our understanding of economic re-generation is!

I have been travelling around the country for the past ten odd days and there is no question that the common man is being hit where it hurts most. Food prices are certainly up no matter what the Finance Minister may say about vitalizing the PDS (public distribution system) around the country. Add to that, the basic costs of all goods that need transportation: while the Prime Minister may be in the Rajya Sabha from the North-East, it is that region that will be the worst hit with these insane increases in aviation fuel not to mention that while there are some states in India that levy a 4% sales tax, there are others that charge a whopping 33%. And guess which are the states that charge this high 33%? The ones ruled by the Congress!

Which is why Amar Singh's stand on this whole political re-alignment is not surprising at all. They, the Samajwadi Party, have been hounded by Mayawati. Therefore they need all the help they can get from the Centre and knowing Amar Singh as I do, he will extract every pound of flesh before he submits to the Congress. Hungry dinner guests rarely forget the humiliation that was once heaped on them.

But where do all these political shenanigans leave India. Well I guess no one is even bothered about this right now. The BJP is still savouring its Karnataka victory whereas the Mayawatis of this world are busy erecting more statues of Kanshi Ram. In a country where the CBI takes more than two months to solve a simple double-murder, are you surprised that we are called the land of the ultimate paradox?

I am not.

8

Why We Need to Call Their Bluff?

There is never going to be a better time than now for the present Government to call the bluff of the Communists and ensure there is a general election. The more this Government dithers, the worse it will be for the UPA in any impending election: not only will they be blamed for incompetence, but worse still, they will be hauled over the coals for indecisiveness. I have often wondered, what is it ion our genetic structure in India, that we always have a reason to make things fail. Just when everything seems to be going right for us, there will be some vested interest which will rear its ugly head and mess things up. It helps no one, and certainly not the country and this is my enduring worry.

The nuclear deal is good for our country. In fact it is going to be possibly the best thing we could ever hope for. We are an energy-scarce country and we need to shore that up if we wish to achieve that 10% GDP growth and the sooner we realize this, the better off we shall be. But no one in the Communist Party understands that only because when was the last time they ever bothered about national interest. They have always been and shall remain insular only because they have so little at stake. There is no question that the Communists will be routed in the next elections. But the reality is they don't care: they have ideological ambitions of converting capitalists to communism. National development is not on their agenda. I sincerely believe this country is blessed because of the Prime Minister we have. By procrastinating on the nuclear deal we are only damaging him further. And more than that, we are damaging our reputation as a sovereign which cannot even keep its word. And that is what the international community thinks of us.

The BJP is also playing the politics of opportunism as they possibly must, given that they too have no clear political philosophy left what with the Ram temple being a thing of the past. The fact that the BJP announces a token list of its potential Lok Sabha candidates is nothing short of a gimmick and it has been viewed thus. The truth of the matter is there are no real issues left and instead of our political parties coming together and harnessing inflation; looking at strengthening our food security our busy imagining the premature demise of a perfectly sound Government. This is where our politicians show themselves up for being the short-sighted selfish people that they really are.

In the past few days, we have witnessed the weakening of this Government. We have seen them go from a working one to being a lame-duck one. There is no reason why this pain must be extended where it actually begins hurting national interest and development. No Prime Minister wishes to be ineffective and this is what the current political environment has done to the Prime Minister. He is too good a man to protest publicly which is why the only solution is to sign the deal, go in for elections and call their bluff. The nation will respond by booting the communists out in an election. That to my mind is the only way forward. The time for prescriptive medicine is over. We now need surgery and need it urgently. In fact the UPA will only weaken its own electoral prospects if it continues to dither. Call their bluff and move on.

9

The Importance of Being Baalu

I cannot imagine the noise we are making about Baalu getting things done for his son. If Nehru could give Indira, India and if all the young ones who are today ministers are results of some fine dynasties, then why are we grudging poor Baalu some gas and that too from an ever-obliging Murli Deora? The truth of the matter is that India is not a country. It is a club and a cosy club at that. Not everyone matters and the sooner you realise this, the better off you will be. The fact of the matter is the ones in power are today no longer in politics alone: they are also in business. Some get into business after they come to power and the others get to power after they have been in business while there are some fine Rajya Sabha MPs who are both in business and power all at the same time.

Baalu was not being dishonest. He was only being plain stupid. He behaved like a clown and he is suffering. In whichever Government he has served, Baalu has been corrupt and that is a well-known fact. No one in this country, not even a rank idiot will tell you that Baalu is honest. That is not what he is well regarded for. But it the impunity that this Cabinet provides people like Baalu is worrying and my belief is that they finally laid out a nice honey-trap for him. There is no question that Baalu has lost the perceptual battle but whether his dark-glasses wearing leader in Chennai will pull the plug remains to be seen. But then again I would not worry too much if Baalu remains. Corruption in politics is now a given. We almost all condone it and turn a blind eye. When Sukh Ram was caught with Rs 3 crores of currency notes ion his house we all smiled and said, look so what but at least he revolutionized the telecom industry. Now let's imagine that Baalu had done an iota of honest work in his life; made some change to our lives; made some dramatic difference, then we too would have forgiven him his son's gas connections but that was not to be. So today we have a senior Cabinet Minister who has been hauled over the coals for nepotism; the system's gaping holes have been bared and all we see is the disruption of Parliament. We see the decline and complete breakdown of morality. We see members of Parliament behaving like goons and thugs. Even that does not worry me.

What shocks me is that not one of these scoundrels, Baalu included, has even made a whisper of an apology. It is their brazenness, which is alarming. It is their I-give-a-damn attitude that will eventually spell doom. This arrogance is something that this country needs to wake up to because this is the new birthmark of political morality in Gandhi's India. There is an air of defiance that is traumatic for the average citizen and these rogues in politics better realise this. This is the kind of behaviour, which leads to violent resolutions. This is what causes anger to come upto the surface and then boil over. This is what the Rang De Basantis are all about. For far too long, we in this country have been made fools of. Which is fine. Our intelligence has been insulted. Which too is fine. Our systems have creaked under the weight of lethargy and corruption. Which too is fine. But then a breaking point comes. When all of the above blend together and when someone, in this case Baalu, cocks a snook at everyone; at the people; at the system; at the political structure and then goes about his work as if nothing ever happened. This is when people snap.

Baalu should worry not about the present. But about the future. Just like Jagdish Tytler and Captain Satish Sharma will never find their way into any Cabinet for completely different reasons, Baalu's tenure too is over. He may last in this Government but he will be in not other. Politicians can live with taint. They cannot live with those who are remorseless.

This is a country, which reveres forgiveness. We love to see our idols being apologetic. For us the desire to escape from an apology smacks of an arrogance that we can never forgive. This is the lesson that Baalu should have learnt. It is quite another matter that the lessons he will learn in future will be more tormentous and severe. But then as they say, it is in his karma.

10

Why India Needs Cheerleaders?

I am amazed at the whole song and dance that is being made on this cheerleading at IPL matches. There are far graver issues that we need to contend with and all we can do is worry about six or seven girls at every match. The truth of the matter is cricket has become another form of entertainment. The reality is that cricket is now more about commerce and less about sport and in any such transition, the first (and perhaps only) thing that merits attention is the consumer and all of this is being done to create heightened consumer awareness and hopefully greater consumer loyalty and I see no harm in that as long as there are clear deliverables from this form of cricket. What anguishes me is the manner in which every one in this country becomes the culture custodian.

This country of ours has had a liberal history so why are we wishing it away. We have nudity in our temples; we have nudity in our monuments; we have had a 3000 year history of Nautch girls and the same people from the BJP who are today talking about culture, have violated every decent humane practice by supporting Godhra when it happened. Why should India's Parliament waste its valuable time discussing cheerleaders when we have issues such as the looming food crisis or for that matter power shortages facing us. The prioritization of issues seems so warped to my mind and this is something that needs course correction.

The fact is that in India today, we have very few things to be excited about and of those, cricket is one. It is now no longer a national sport. It has become a national obsession and the attempt to create clubs of cricket just like football clubs in the United Kingdom is something that is here to stay. As the federation splinters over issues such as water-sharing and linguistic patterns, we will also see regional pride surfacing through these cricket clubs and once again there is no harm in this. The deeper issue is whether this form of cricket will inject greater investment into sporting infrastructure and that to my mind is something that should bother us. Our stadia wear a tired look. They are woefully inadequate as far as any consumer conveniences are concerned. Eden Gardens even had a power failure while the match was going on. This pitiable state of affairs needs to change. The administrators of sports in this country need to give back far more than they take from sponsors and government alike. You cannot have a situation where the sports body gets richer and the infrastructure poorer. That is just not on.

As for the IPL, the timing could not have been better. There is certainly a lot of excitement around this and my guess is, they will be able to sustain it. And one of the vital ingredients, whether we like it or not, will be the cheerleaders. They have an important role to play and the tragedy is the politicians just don't seem to understand. Equating cheerleaders with bar girls is silly and illogical. By that logic Rakhee Sawant should also be banned, as should Aishwarya Rai for doing her item number. The thing we need to worry about is not cheerleaders destroying our culture but instead politicians messing us up by their lack of ethics and values. That is the greater worry.

All said and done, it is not very often that we get opportunities to celebrate in our country. Now that we have one such as the IPL, let us not be cynical and inward looking. India's culture is not so fragile that it will crumble by the moves of some cheerleaders. Let us be more mature, and at times a bit more intelligent.

(Suhel Seth is Managing Partner of Counselage: suhel@counselage.com)

11

Organ Failure

For Ambumani Ramadoss, who makes periodic noises over consumption of tobacco and fights with competent directors of medical institutes, there is an eerie silence every time something of the magnitude as the kidney racket is exposed and one wonders if there is any one really in charge of the Health Ministry in this country or are we seeing the same kind of posturing that is all bluster and no deed. The fact that you have quacks functioning with gay abandon is known to each of us. That is only because there is no real healthcare strategy that either this very voluble minister or his bureaucrats have in the ministry. Our primary healthcare model is in a shambles and today India, despite its much touted GDP growth actually has a declining health standard simply because those who matter can afford private healthcare and those who can't just don't matter to this aam aadmi government.

I have constantly believed that we cannot be at every forum from Davos to Singapore going hoarse about our economic prowess if we cannot even provide basic health facilities in our country to those who need it all the time. The fact that you have private healthcare available should send a signal to the Government that it is not talent that we lack, but the will to plan and execute. I have been observing the constant utterances of this minister and they always seem to be in the domain of populism but never address the real issues that face the people of this country. Tobacco is a scourge and there are no two views about this but surely a cabinet minister must be doing more than appealing to Bollywood stars to achieve what he believes are national goals. Here again, big tobacco is almost an island unto itself and there will never be any way that you can rein them in. They will use every trick in the book to flog their value and existence: from farmers to real value-added pricing for commodities, which in any case they control. The moot point lies somewhere between. We have to have a national policy towards all such issues be it HIV or for that matter unabated tobacco consumption and by just having a Nafisa Ali or for that matter a Shahrukh Khan, we are not going to address the eradication in a serious way. What we will be left with is another bout of rampant tokenism which again this minister is very good at.

I am not even going into the merits of the drama at AIIMS but there is no question in my mind that we have now politicized the finest medical institution beyond repair and all key parties are to blame including the judiciary, which shouldn't have interfered. But once again the damage has been done and there is no one accountable. The facilities at AIIMS are in a mess and unless you are a VIP, there is no hope of any decent medical care that you can expect. If you move beyond Delhi and go to state capitals, the situation is even more alarming. The state of Bihar is reeling as far as medical care is concerned and the irony is that more doctors in AIIMS come from Bihar than any other state and yet in their own backyard there is no facility where they can put their impeccable talent to good use. The same is the condition in West Bengal. I have now learnt that even the venerable Breach Candy Hospital in Bombay will be headed by a person whose past track-record is suspect. So while the minister goes to town over cigarette smoking, the 87% of smokers who consume bidis are left out because of vested interest and political influence not to mention those who consumer other forms of tobacco such as gutka and pan Masala. Which means once again, we've missed the woods for the trees and there is nothing anyone wishes to do. I have yet to see a robust document from the Planning Commission on the healthcare strategy for our country going forward. There is no segmentation plan either which carefully delineates the three pillars of any healthcare system: primary, secondary or tertiary. Our entire preventive healthcare system is amiss. The communication on most diseases is absent and it almost post facto that we take any steps causing even greater pain to both citizens and the exchequer alike.

I sincerely believe the Prime Minister needs to focus his attention on the kind of people he has reposed faith in, to solve (or address) India's healthcare needs. The present incumbent has done precious little except to appear on television imploring actors instead of industry to act. The focus itself is misplaced and that needs to be corrected. There is no point in telling the world we're a great economic power if our very health is suspect! It is much like the state we are in today: operation successful, patient dead!

12

A Mouthful of Syrupy Management

Shombit Sengupta is undoubtedly a man of colour: a Bengali to boot who had adapted to his adopted country, France much like a Bengali takes to fish. But it is the curiously titled 'Jalebi Management' that unravels the tubular structure as Sen (this is what they call him in Europe he tells us) calls it of life in the world of management.

Jalebi Management is a fascinating book only because it is written by someone who has never run companies; in fact, Sengupta only advises them and his advise is largely in the design area therefore what you get is a very basic overview of management honed by the years that Sengupta has spent between Calcutta where he landed up as a refugee torn by religious separatism as he calls it and then on went to Paris where Zidane-like, he came to terms with 15 Franc jalebis and the whole midnight revelry which Algerians committed in a city not entirely theirs.

The essential premise of the book is pithy and true. The world of management is increasingly getting to be more and more riddled with complexity and discomfort with the status quo is something that should delight (and not scare) the CEO because from this discomfort arises the need to do something about it. Status quo breeds complacency which is what we see missing in today's competitive environment which is why he begins brilliantly with the million versus billion mindset arguing that a million-mindset (the Americas and Europe) can never understand the needs; the pressures and the aspirations of the billion-mindset people (china and India) almost presenting a case why we in India must be content with a Shatabdi Express rather than aspire to a TGV as in his native France.

And in this journey to present life in the world of management as a Jalebi, Sengupta covers a lot of ground. In fact, I believe a little too much. The reader travels from the travails of the 14th District of Paris to the epic film 'The Dreamer' which Bertolucci produced in 2003 to talk about an evolving society with greater permissiveness and here Sengupta argues, lies the same analogies qua management. There are various kinds of promoters and different sets of values that drive companies. From the kind of promoter who is god to the kind of company that is Apple.

Where the book scores tremendously is the broad brush-strokes of social engineering coupled with Sengupta's own views on all that impact us, which he is able to transmit succinctly. Thus the theories of management are no longer theories. In fact the book becomes a delicious bite rather than remain a forbidding fruit. Tempting but self-defeating. There is an obvious French bias in the book: almost all examples gave their origins in France. Be it the re-interpretation of the art of Egypt as reflected in I M Pei's glass pyramid outside the Louvre to the changes that have been witnessed in French culture to the visible architecture of Place Pompidou. The brilliance of Sengupta's book lies in the fact that it is management made both easy and if I may add very edible. It could only be a

Bengali settled in Paris who would extend his pining for jalebis to the title of a management book,

Unlike most management books, the examples transcend the routine company case-studies and are instead historical truths on the one hand and researched experiences on the other which is why the book is as practical as perhaps eating a jalebi as is complex making one. But then Sengupta has always been the maverick that the general world of advertising and marketing has frowned upon for his avant-garde style. I like his comments on the need for renovation and his indictment of the Indian Establishment for unwilling to look at scientific renovations of heritage.

The good thing is that this book of his tells us he hasn't changed. This is a must-read book. If nothing else, it is a perfect ode to the humble jalebi!

(Suhel Seth is Managing Partner of Counselage India: suhel@counselage. com)

13

And Justice for All?

I for one cannot fathom the depths to which the process of equitable justice in this country has fallen! It is indeed sad that every person who is able to, fiddles with the justice system in whichever manner he can and there is nothing that can be done about it. There is no question that Manu Sharma wouldn't be behind bars if the Delhi High Court hadn't stepped in: somehow the law enforcement arms such as the police are either inept or corrupt or both and we have seen repeated incidents of this malaise. The Alistair Pereira case in Bombay is reprehensible to say the least: the BMW case in Delhi is no better but the justice system has been so tweaked that there is almost a brazenness with which people who have killed people can get away.

I guess the malaise is deeper than you and I think: I do not believe we have the kind of judges at lower levels that we need: they are supported by weak prosecution processes with the result that it easy to subvert the system and get away with blue murder. I am tired of being told that the police messed up the investigations and therefore the guilty have gotten away scott-free: this is not on and the fact that we have to listen to this drivel from some sessions judge makes matters only worse. What we are unleashing is a terror state where anyone can do whatever the hell they want with the law and then get away wither because they've fixed the system or for that matter the lower sessions judicial process and we are seeing it again and again!

For a country that has to constantly rely on the media to raise issues of equitable justice is a sad commentary on our criminal justice system and from what one sees and reads, there will never be an effort by the concerned people to actually overhaul the criminal justice system.

You can have a college professor murdered in broad daylight by some political thugs and yet you can't bring those scoundrels to justice only because the system is so rotten from within that it will not allow their prosecution: this is a telling testimony to the so-called independence of the judiciary that we are so constantly reminded of. I believe any country, which allows the Manu Sharmas of the world to roam around till a vigilant media raises a storm, is not a country that can ever talk about justice and the law. It simply doesn't exist. And why should the judges sacrifice their role at the altar of hyped media only to render eventual justice? My belief is that had the media not raised the issue of Jessica Lal's death going unpunished, there would have been no remedial action so in a manner while the Delhi High Court did a superlative job, in a strange way they abrogated their role to media vigilantes rather than rightfully strong judicial intervention and herein lies the paradox within the Indian state as it were! Because the very same media that is concerned about justice could very well get busy with some silly wedding and the concerned criminal could get away scot-free besides of course the view that the media cannot actually brand people guilty till they are proven so. So there are a host of contradictions in the very system that we need to manage withy compassion and urgency.

But then this Government is so busy with OBCs and with Rahul Gandhi re-writing military history that I do not believe we will ever see a dramatic and fundamental change in the justice system that we so desperately need. Add to this the fees that lawyers are charging nowadays, you have a lethal concoction which will ensure either way the one seeking justice dies: of bankruptcy of money and/or ideas.

14

An Officer and a Gentleman

First a set of disclosures: I have never owned nor ever will, a single share or any stock. I do not invest in mutual funds or any such thing. I abhor the stock markets since I believe they are generally the preserve of scamsters and such like. I also believe that we haven't done enough to give people like Ketan Parekh demonstrable punishment for duping innocent investors but then that is the tragedy with out judicial system. I blame the stock markets for creating easy money for people to play around with and drive up prices of essentials like housing and so on. I know of several friends who, even while making love, are checking out prices of which stock has moved and why? My only investments are in bank fixed deposits.

Which is why it was such a pleasure to spend an anecdote-laced coffee session with M K Damodaran, the Chairman of SEBI: like me, he too owns no shares or any investments in mutual funds and everything you hear about his avowed integrity is true. The good news for the average investor is just this: that Damodaran is responsible for their interests as Chairman of SEBI. Which is why high profile IPOs for large real-estate companies have gotten stuck, as have errant brokers and so on. Shivnath Thukral of NDTV mentioned how one such real-estate company from Bombay invited their journalists to Mauritius to see them at work. This is the change that India needs in more areas than just regulating the capital markets. Take a look at the recent past: you've had several companies list at much lower prices than their IPO offering price and who gets burnt the most? The hapless investor. It is clear that most of the companies that are going to market have enough guile in them to engineer communication in a manner, which will make them come across as smelling of roses. Shivnath Thukral of NDTV Profit mentioned how one such real-estate company from Bombay invited their journalists to Mauritius to see them at work. Then you have companies that stuff their boards with so-called heavy-weight names hoping that those heavy-hitters will be ammunition enough to both convince regulators as also the investor as to why investing in their companies will make for sound economic sense. I believe this country needs more people like Damodaran only for one reason: they have the courage to push reforms and yet never sacrifice their integrity which is so sorely lacking in almost everything around us and what Damodaran told me in that one hour of blissful conversation at his spanking new office is that the system of governance in India is not a deterrent if you don't want it to be! And this is the essential point. There are many good people in the system and there are many amongst the youth in this country that still believe in serving in Government.

I was quite surprised, as I am sure you will be too, at knowing that SEBI is the only Government body which is a Day Zero company at two IIM campuses: Bangalore and Calcutta and a Day One company at Ahmedabad and Lucknow. And the pride with which Damodaran says this is something worth cherishing. He believes, as most of us should that there are lots of people today who are willing to take compensation cuts and work for the larger interest of the nation. The fact that two IIM students that Damodaran recruited from IIM are getting an annual compensation of cost-to-company of Rs 6 lakhs versus the offer that these very students got from a London-based investment bank of Rs 72 lakhs per annum is an indicator not jut of how they've got their hearts in the right place but I would imagine is a quiet testimony to Damodaran's leadership skills as well. It was not surprising therefore to learn from him that he never allows anyone but himself to handle the HR portfolio.

I have often said that this country needs to respect and reward good people: there are enough in the system who need to become the role models that this system otherwise never allows them to become. There was a clear energy that one saw during our coffee session: there was no rancour only unbridled optimism.

And when you have the kind of volatility that exists in this market; when you have so many people who work without scruples in our capital markets, you need someone who you can not only respect but also fear. And the ability to strike fear only comes when you have nothing to gain or lose from either influence or some power-hungry politician but it was Damodaran's take on politicians that impressed me the most. He recounted an anecdote of how when he was a young District Magistrate in Tripura, he had to arrest the then leader of opposition, the formidable communist, Nripen Chakraborty. By the time Nripen Chakraborty became Chief Minister, Damodaran has been posted to some other District but was summoned to the state capital upon which he feared the worst: that he would be given a punishment posting. But instead, Chakraborty invited him to serve as his own Secretary which Damodaran declined because his task in the District was still unfinished upon which the CM asked him to suggest a name: the moot point being that the politician always knows good officers from bad.

I sometimes believe that people like Damodaran need to be cloned: for the good of this country if for nothing else. And there are many like him. But it is always the unsung that are also easily forgotten. I only hope Damodaran goes on to do more than SEBI when the time comes. It is another matter that we didn't discuss cricket but then a victory over Bermuda hardly makes for inspiring conversation!

15

A History of Violence?

Has Ahmisa finally given way in this country of ours? Have we adopted the barbarism that was once the hallmark of the Wild West? Is Indian culture now headed towards a new reality where beating to death beats all other forms of recrimination and punishment? Have we emerged from the closet as a society that really is fractured so deeply that intolerance has become our birthmark?

What happened to Professor Sabharwal in Ujjain last week is a shame. A shame not because a man was killed but also because that venerable relationship between student and teacher was destroyed forever only because some goons (the BJP's youth wing ABVP) killed him without remorse and care. This is happening in our country with alarming regularity. Our intolerance levels are rising with each passing day and there perhaps needs to be some introspection to understand why we have become like this. What is so wretched in our lives that we value life so little? What is happening to our social construct that we are willing to demolish homes and happiness only to prove a silly political point? This intolerance has many facets. It is seen in the form of endless personal vilification and abuse in Parliament. It is seen in the brutality of the police who leave no stone unturned to be harsh and unkind when they just need to follow the law. We are seeing this in the revival of bloody caste wars and so on and so forth,

We are seeing this in our schools and colleges. Temples of learning have become temples of death. We are observing this in the casual manner in which terrorists are going about their task and all we can do is discuss the aftermath on television and in newspapers. What happened in Ujjain will happen elsewhere as well. It will happen in our own backyard because that tragically has become the norm rather than the exception. And we are to blame.

Our judges are to blame. Our police are to blame and our politicians have long been the cause of this. It is sad that while on the one hand, we have many reasons to be proud of our judiciary, and there are instances with regard to the Criminal Procedure Code, which are worthy of shame. We have done nothing to bring in reforms in this most crucial area and there is almost a feeling amongst the rich and the powerful that they can get away. And the tragedy is they do. Every time a criminal walks free, it is a slur on India's judicial system and on its complete helplessness. It is a testimony to the fact that no matter what you might say, even the judiciary is kinder to the one who has money and influence. In which other country would you take 13 years to dispense justice in a bomb blast case? In which country would a Manu Sharma cock a snook in our faces and roam with the freedom of a honourable man? Which country would exonerate those accused of corruption and scams. Recently I saw Ketan Parekh travelling business class from Delhi to Mumbai with impunity. Last year he was a guest at Wildflower Hall in Shimla. The man who tore down the co-operative banking system is now a messiah, all over again.

You have criminals in Parliament and that is supposed to be the place where laws are framed. You have criminals in the Union Cabinet and that is the place, which is supposed to run this country. You have police officers that get the gallantry award on August 15 and are arrested for bribery on August 29. This is the farce that is being played out day after day and it is convenient for every one to remain quiet. You cannot object to the vandalisation of the Ridge by big business and big organisations only because they have followed the diktat of the DDA, which is a known corrupt organisation. My question is don't these builders and corporations have a conscience? Don't we need to worry about the environmental damage that we are causing to Delhi by developing the Ridge?

We can all pretend to be the world's greatest democracy. We can all cry hoarse about the freedom of the press and the freedom of the judiciary. We can all tom-tom the long arm of the law and how efficient our laws are to book the corrupt and the evil. But my question is what respect do we really have when we see the rascals who caused Prof Sabharwal's death running free? What respect do we have for the Government when we see a Shibu Soren back in the Cabinet? What respect to do we have for the system when we see Manu Sharma entertaining diners at his eatery in Chandigarh?

In this rush towards progress we are slowly destroying those simple values that guided us at one time. Is it a good thing or a bad thing? Well look around and you can gauge for yourself!

16

An Open Letter to the Speaker

Dear Somnath Da:

It is time you took some serious action against erring MPs and actually threw some of them out from the hallowed precincts of Parliament for the shame that some of them have heaped on this institution is not worthy of enduring. It is sad we have a bunch of hoodlums who indulge in the worst form of loutish behaviour and hold no truck for basic decency.

Is this what we want the children of today's India to grow up to? Is this the kind of parliamentary democracy we wish to engender where people abuse each other's mother and level allegations which are not only disgusting but epitomize a sick mind? What happened on the 23rd of August was despicable: just at the time when India enters its 60th year of independence. Is this what our founding fathers envisaged for a place, which would protect the freedom and the rights of millions of Indians? We have for long debated the fact that some of our MPs are an absolute shame who tend to hide behind privileges and take part in the worst kind of carnages of basic decency. If this is the India that will be projected on national television then you can kiss respect goodbye.

Whether you like it or not, Parliament today is a shamed institution in the eyes of many. It is a shame that last week

MPs gave themselves a salary hike at a time when their performance itself is under the scanner. Man-hours in Parliament are lost only because of the lack of seriousness that some of these MPs exhibit. I was watching television when on one occasion you actually had to admonish (in absence) the Union Health Minster since he did not turn up to address the House. If this is the kind of MPS we wish to have, then of what use is this white elephant?

People outside the houses of Parliament actually ridicule the institution that it has become today. Is this the legacy that this current House wishes to leave behind? A legacy of indecency; of indecision and of inexcusable behaviour. One in which the focus is more on exchanging angry words rather than debating legislation? The general public at one time looked up to Parliament. It had what one would term social sanction. Today it suffers from social ostracisation. And that is something that will destroy this institution as time goes by and this is what perhaps you need to stem.

The very MPs who rush into the well whenever they have nothing intelligent to say are the ones who will lead this decline and nothing is being done to stop them. We've had many incidents of shame and utter disgust but the fact that a Union Minister could take part in a slanging match was the true nadir of this august body! Will any of this ever change? I don't think it can. The pedigree of some of the MPs of today is an issue. If you elect criminals and rogues to our Parliaments, as some of them are, then this is the kind of quorum you will get and it is now beginning to show. What respect does Parliament earn when the police want some of its members? What real respect? When I look back at what the institution really was, it saddens me even more. From the stirring speeches of Pandit Nehru and the wit of Piloo Mody we have now fallen to the heckling of cabinet ministers and mindless abuses by corrupt MPs. Is this the kind of Parliament we wish to have?

The Central Hall is no longer a centre for debate but has instead become a large waiting room for the elite who feed on subsidized food. Nothing more. The truth of the matter is no one would grudge our MPs their free telephone calls and subsidized food as long as some real work was getting done. But even that has stopped. It is tragic that at a time when one of Brand India's value propositions to the world is THE GREATEST FREE MARKET DEMOCRACY, the very institution that can and must guarantee this is under the scanner.

It is indeed sad that some MPs, and a small number at that, have laid siege on our Parliament and brought it to a stage where some of us may very well question its moral right to govern this country. Or for that matter pass legislation. When was the last time, you head of intelligent legislation being drafted and discussed by people whose real home should have been a prison.

The time for you sir to purge has arrived. You need to take action that will be both demonstrable and serve as a deterrent. Time is truly running out.

India's Parliament is slowly moving from zero hour to near zero relevance.

17

A Nation in the Well!

If someone had told me even five years ago, that this country would be seized one weekend over a little fellow falling into a bore-well, I would have laughed. But then whoever said India is bereft of surprises. It must be terrible times for this country which on the one hand is attempting to launch rockets and missiles and on the other cannot even prevent people from falling into freshly dug wells. To make matters worse, I was subjected to a barrage of television on an issue, which is not just silly but does not even deserve the attention it finally got.

I was also aghast to see an economic daily then conjecture whether Prince will finally get endorsements and if he will be a greater draw than Tendulkar and Dhoni. Have we as a nation completely lost it? Do we have nothing else to do? Is the media so intellectually bankrupt or riddled with TRP greed that we now have to be forced to see a little fellow feeding on biscuits and chocolates? I was in Goa with a very acclaimed television personality who got a message from some Nachiket fellow to say that Renuka Choudhury had just declared an award for Prince for Rs 2 lakhs and that if any further clarifications were needed (which means a TV interview) the minister was available. Are we finally living in cuckoo-land or what? Why on earth would Renuka offer an award of Rs 2 lakhs to some fellow who falls into a well? If this is not tokenism, then what is? Renuka must have been very ill advised to even make this offer since the media has seen through it. Just like they have seen through the offer of help, which the Haryana Chief Minister offered: he told camera-crews that he was going to fly in teams from Holland and Germany to rescue Prince. Why doesn't Hooda do something about the roads and the infrastructure, which allows for these mishaps to occur? Am I missing something or are we really being governed by those bordering on complete lunacy?

The real issues are no longer important which is why they never get highlighted. The Vidarbha farmer is now akin to hockey reportage so it has fallen off the map. No one is talking about the 500,000 farmers that have committed suicide till date. The media is not interested in pillorying the men and women who disrupt Parliament or for that matter ripping Jaswant Singh apart for the irresponsible statements he makes as if he were teaching Keats to a bunch of students at the college he never went to: Oxford. Jaswant's casual remarks have to be seen in the light of the collateral damage that they do to both the institution of the PMO as also to our diplomatic ties with the United States. If Rupa wants to sell more copies of his books they need to employ better marketing techniques and not sensationalism.

The issues of social justice and government interference in educational institutions has also fallen off the media radar. This is the time when the ugly mind of Arjun Singh will rise again and my worry is that the media will just not notice.

In India today, reality television has replaced real television. In financial papers there was time when you saw graphs and pie-charts: today you see Superman and cartoon characters. If the dumbing down is not complete, pray tell me how more stupid do we need to get.

The Mumbai blasts will soon be forgotten as will all the development work that Mumbai so desperately needs. I am afraid closer home, in Delhi, the Ridge will yield forest land to luxury malls and no one seems to care. I sometimes wonder if there is any hope even from the judiciary. In a country where retired judges are made Chairmen of various Commissions, how can we inspire enduring faith amongst the common man? These are the issues that must seize us: not some fellow falling into a well. The Indian Army doesn't need to be congratulated for pulling out a 6 year old boy from a well in Haryana. They need to ensure that cross-border terrorism ends and we don't have people walking across into India as if they were taking a post-dinner walk.

No one is ever going to check when Lakshmi Mittal will finally invest in India: promises are one thing and parting with the cheque quite another. In the capital we have insurmountable woes be it power or water. So how on earth does it matter if the Government of India has managed to pull out a boy from a well.

When are they going to pull the nation and EACH of its constituents out of this mess? So that farmers stop killing themselves and people don't have to ride trains of death. But then don't expect too much from the media. They are busy inventing the next candle. Not the real issues!

18

A Saga Steeped in Literary Blood

To describe M. J. Akbar's 'Blood Brothers' as an autobiography would be limiting its realm of influence. To call it a work of fiction would put it in a genre that would again restrict the vastness of the expanse the book covers. The book can best be described as a multi-parallel work of literature, if ever there was one. The book runs across three planes with equal felicity: on the one plane, it is an account of the family that gave birth to M J Akbar; on another it is a telling and insightful story of India's multi-culturalism especially the constant contrasts that we draw between Hindus and Muslims and finally, on yet another plane, it is an account of India's history told not by a historian but by someone who grew up with a life that was touched and in many ways severely impacted by the turn of events that India experienced during its fight for freedom.

But it is not just the account that seems to hold till the very end. Books often have single heroes: much like Hollywood films: but it is here, that Akbar, much like the Bollywood he reveres (and is so often mentioned in the book: from Sharmila Tagore's bikini to the debate whether Mother India should have been a Hindu or a Muslim) has done more than just woven an intricate story. He has peppered it with literary standards honed over the years and in an environment, which encouraged craft with equal fervour as it did the plot. To that end, Akbar's book is a delightful read. It is a window not just into societal norms that were prevalent over the last three centuries but in many ways talks about the harmony that India never lost despite what happened both as a run-up to freedom, and after. It is here where the book scores amazingly.

It is a personal account, which tells a larger story: explaining the meaning of life to a man who was growing up in a time when you were either known by the religion you belonged to or by the wealth you had. What is more interesting is the anecdotal pace that Akbar brings to the book: from describing his grandfather's death, which reads, "My grandfather died while I was playing on his chest. That was my first stroke of luck" to paragraphs which capture the hypocrisy of the babu brigade that was prevalent in Bengal. There is the famous letter that Baboo Satyajit Banerjee writes inviting his English friends to a night of whoring which is actually couched as an invitation to see Nautch. Which means dance.

It is also a book that has an underlying resilience: that of a man whose family, much like Indian families today, paid a premium on their child's education. Riveting are the anecdotes that tell us about Akbar's education: first at the tony Calcutta Boys School and then again at Presidency College where Akbar gets his first real lessons in life. It is this ability to weave incidents that are paradoxical, that make Blood Brothers such a compelling read. Even the dedication in the book tells a story. Akbar dedicates this book to his children Mukulika and Prayaag. Prayaag was also the name of Akbar's grandfather: it is almost as if life for Akbar has come a full circle.

There are also early signals in the form of anecdotes that Akbar regales us with which has a lot to with his current profession as a journalist. Te struggle with the 'Letter to the Editor' of The Statesman make for some delightful reading and do give us a window into the world of journalism that is now perhaps non-existent.

It is a saga that is steeped in emotion but an emotion which is unique to Akbar: there is a thoroughness of research that imparts broad-spectrum wisdom: from learning about the man who invented nicotine, to the founder of condoms, all find a place in this book. From the art of circumcision to the art of being circumspect in English company, there is a tale told with fondness and finesse which is what makes Blood Brothers such a fine book and a compelling read. One, which has something for everyone, I would imagine.

I would even hesitate to add, that this is perhaps Akbar's finest book yet.

Suhel Seth is Managing Partner of Counselage India.

19

Shubho Pujo: Surviving the Goddess...

For me, the Pujas is perhaps the most emotional of all festivals and I am certain that this column will receive more than its fair share of comments and concerns so, rather than wait for the deluge, here is a survival guide to the Pujas. Read this and you will need to do nothing more except vegetate during the festival: you can keep a copy of this guide handy when you are at the local pandal watching women whilst ostensibly seeking some divine intervention. Or for that matter you can print copies and charge for it rather than just indulge in mild extortion and give them the baloney that you are doing it for the goddess. This is the time when the Goddess takes prime place; Buddhadev and Bhutia will vanish from our lives and thank God for that. Instead the *para mastaan* and the affable traffic policeman will replace them. Suddenly, the women who you never thought much of ever will start looking like supermodels so you have to handle that with care. You must make it a point to compliment every boudi who steps out of her home and into the larger world. You must comment on their beautiful hair and their lovely eyes. Every boudi has remarkable eyes since they spend almost their entire life weeping at their choice of husband. This is the time for you to move in. If you are a bachelor, then the Pujas are the most critical phase of your annual existence. This is the time you can either score or go back to playing cards at the local teashop. This is the time when you have to tell the world you have arrived and it does help if you suddenly brush up on Tagore and Amartya. The average Bengali girl still swoons over intellect: unlike the average Punjabi girl who will only love diamonds as long as they can be worn at someone else's cost.

It will help if you also brush up on your knowledge of the pujas and the traditions that bind it. Don't panic when you hear the drumbeats. They are not shooting Mangal Pandey, The Falling. You must also remember to tell the world that you were awake when All India Radio was broadcasting the Mahalaya program: nothing inspires people to respect you more when you tell them you are a man of their time. Not just your own. Be kind to your dhobi during the Pujas. I have seen men and women being destroyed by their dhobis or for that matter by the lack of starch on what they wear. Remember a crisply starched dress is your passport to success. You also need to be careful of the kind of things you are found eating once in the pandal. My submission is eat less and drink more. The more you drink, the better off you will be. That way you will tolerate the noise levels as also the pollution. Coca Cola is always the best option. If you want to be truly macho, then try Thums Up. If all you want, is to charm a few snakes, then try Pepsi. Remember the pujas are the ultimate test of control. You will need to control the passing of the wind. You will need to control that inevitable burp and you will need to control being truthful. This is the time when you need to be nice to every one. Just plaster a plastic smile and it will not harm you: look at what a smile can get you: from the aunty of the para to the beauty queen of the para who still believes in Boroline and Kashundi mustard. These are the moments you need to savour.

My other submission is, no matter which gender you belong to, align your forces early. Which is why it is critical to stop working long before the pujas begin and do some basic research. Find out who will be in Calcutta and who will not. Then start making necessary preparations: it may help in ingratiating yourself with the him and her you are really keen on. Remember it is the first day, just like the first impression, that makes all the difference. If on Sapthami, you aren't scoring, then you might as well plan your own *bisarjan* along with that of the goddess' because others would have taken over by then. Remember to be very respectful towards your parents. This is the time when you and your family have to be role models in the locality. The *para* needn't know that your mother's favorite dish for your father is a *kobiraji cultet* laced with rat poison. The secrets of your family need to be well guarded which is why it is essential you step out every evening with one parent on either side. If you have only one parent or none, you will be at a slight handicap though having no parent at all may equally get you the sympathy vote. And then do things that girls love in men. They love men bowing to touch the feet of elders, which is why you must practice this movement to a fine art. The trick is to bend, but bend sideways: that way you don't have to go down all the way and it also seems more dramatic and is more visible in a crowd. Do these kinds of things: they make women melt with delight.

The pujas are also a time to reflect: on how to get smarter. On how to raise community money for personal needs; on how to become a mastaan by never raising your finger and if everything works out well, then how to actually enjoy the pujas without ever seeing the goddess. But if I were you, I would ignore all of the above and let my heart do whatever it wishes to. Because for me, it is only during the Pujas, that Kolkata comes alive. We leave behind the pain and the sorrows that effect our daily life; we revel in the arrival of the goddess and we experience a tinge of sadness when she departs but one, which is laced, with the optimism of her impending return the next year.

The drumbeats I have heard during the Pujas when I was growing up in Kolkata were akin to the heartbeat of a city, which thankfully is still the most civilised in our country. Where people have not replaced humanity and where the goddess comes year after year to bless her own and to celebrate the hues and colours of life with her devotees. Perhaps the most striking element about the pujas is that it allows the beauteous to rise above the ordinary and in that transition allows each one of us to aspire to greater good. That to my mind is the eternal contribution of the Pujas to Kolkata!

20

The Food that Commoners Eat!

I have often been asked by friends and foes whether street food is something that must be encouraged: not just as an option to devour but equally as an option to savour and I must confess I have ever felt more definitive I my answer. There is no better food than genuine street food, which is why people like Vijay Goel are so popular since they serve it all the time in their homes. The next time you are at a banquet, observe how quickly people queue up for the cholaa-tikkis or the chillads or even the common alu-chaat. These are delicacies in the truest sense. Of the many reasons why I still love to live in Delhi is the abundance of great street food here. If you haven't tried the Amritsari kulcha with their superb accompaniment of cholaas and pickled onions, then my friend you haven't lived. If you haven't lost your way to find the dream kathi at Nizam's tucked away in Lajpat Nagar, then you haven't existed. This is food fit for the kings!

My best encounters with food have been with street food and food which you have to seek out. Street food can be very mystifying so don't go looking for the nearest counter or handcart that you spot. There is a charm, almost ethereal in nature, of finding out where you can get the best of the best. Have you ever been to Galina's at Gole Market for their wonderful seekh kababs with rumali rotis? Have you ever taken a trip to Old Delhi and not gone to Karim's but instead to Gullu Meatwalah and tried his mutton with chapattis? I can bet you haven't for the simple reason that most people are risk-averse when it comes to the sampling of food options.

There can be no better start to a Sunday if you don't make that pilgrimage to Chaini Ram and have his amazing puris served with heavenly alu. This is the kind of Sunday to which odes are written. And once you've topped it with sweet lassi, all you need is a fine bed to while away the rest of your Sunday. And when evening sets in, take a round of traffic-less Connaught Place and settle down at National Dhaba and enjoy the keema-egg curry but remember to douse that with tons of onions. I have always then crossed the street from National Dhaba and washed down this heavy meal with an equally enchanting Nutty Buddy from Nirula's. Thank god they haven't tinkered with this as yet!

To my mind Jaya Jaitly has done yeoman service not just to the crafts movement in India but equally to the food culture as well. If anyone goes to Dilli Haat and doesn't try the food, then he's lost the plot. If you are fond of good food, then Dilli Haat it is. But do it the way I do. Head straight for the Bijoli Grill stall and order yourself two dishes: first the mutton cutlet (and for this I always carry buttered bread and chilli sauce from home) after which settle down to devour the Moghlai Paratha which is basically a more civilized egg-paratha but with amazing flavour. Once done, then head for the Mizoram stall and pick on some momos. Washed down with some fruit beer, which you can pick up at the Haryana stall. Trust the jats to think of fruit beer!

I have often been asked where the best kababs can be had. If you have the clout, then telephone Ashwini at Moti Mahal, Greater Kailash M Block Market at about 12 noon and tell him to marinate the burras especially for you at dinner and then go ahead and taste the finest mutton burras that money and hunger can buy. There is yet another place where you can get amazing kababs provided you can stomach the stench: that's the Sardarji Dhaba in Malkaganj which is the iron scrap market, just a few kilometers from Dhaula Kuan. They have unarguably the finest kababs. But sadly enough, they are only open for lunch. And if its butter chicken, then the world's best butter chicken is at Mughal Mahal, at Rajendra Place, a furlong away from Hotel Siddharth. I can vouch for the fact that once you've had butter chicken at Mughal Mahal, there's no place else in the world that you will ever look towards for this fabled Dilli dish!

Street food is amazing so go ahead and seek their divine forms out. There is more character, more taste and more authenticity in street food tan you can get either at home or in a hotel. But as I said, this is for the brave-hearted. Don't try any of the above if you are a fashion model, anorexic or worried about stomach bugs. What's street food without its share of flies and dust? Not to mention the occasional drop of perspiration!

21

The India We Need to Build

The India we need to build cannot be an India, which we can conveniently dub a knowledge-driven nation brand because my premise in this matter is that we do not have an enduring competitive advantage in this domain. We only have a cost advantage for the time being till another country can match the fees we charge for the much-touted BPO successes or for that matter our software prowess. I will admire the Infosys' of the world the day they can create a software brand on the lines of a Window: That is when the Indian brand in the software category can be truly built but while we wait for that to happen, there is enough scope for the Indian brand as it were. I believe tomorrow's Brand India will be built on what we ca do for the world in terms of tourism and agri-driven businesses. Companies like one tobacco major on the one had with their echoupal (wiring the farmer and creating an online commodity exchange as it were) and another major pharmaceutical company with their foray into major research can use the knowledge abundance we speak of to build competitive advantages in the twin areas of food products and pharma products. The other area where tremendous work is possible in the branding of our crafts. My belief is that Brand India will emerge from critical values that are so unique to

India: we are a nation of entrepreneurial drive: look at the top ten businesses in India and they are all almost first generation businesses. It is this spirit of entrepreneurship that needs to be inculcated and tragically this can never be taught at business schools and such like. We need to modify our education process to include a large degree of lateral thinking; innovation of business techniques and basically reinvent the individual. As a corollary, what India needs to sustain this entrepreneurship is better licensing ad approval norms: unlike what we did to SSIs; we need better forms of funding and perhaps the State needs to set up venture capital funding streams which will incubate projects which have this rare entrepreneurial drive.

Infact the cornerstone of India and every Indian is entrepreneurship: the mantra to market this brand facet of ours could well be: The Great Indian Dreamer's Reality. We as a nation have to accept the fact that entrepreneurs must and do fail: it is also imperative for tomorrow's India to accept risk-taking as a natural process of evolution.

The marketing of this brand must however be done cohesively and this is our tragedy. We are terrible marketers and our Government has no clue either. Look at what we did to Darjeeling tea? Until the recent Incredible India campaign, we were weak on tourism marketing. We do not understand global positioning and that cannot be left to the CIIs and FICCIs of the world alone: they are doing a tremendous job but you need more brand ambassadors and you need consistency in your positioning: both of which we lack. The much-touted Brand Equity Fund is unutilized even now. We in India are great at spotting opportunities of global competitive advantage and then too happy to surrender their ownership to someone else.

Time magazine puts Yoga classes in Midwestern America on their cover, not the ones in Benares!

Brand India needs better brand custodians and not politicians and bureaucrats pretending to be brand managers. The day we change the team on the brand, we shall capture the world. As a robust value-proposition brand that is. One which tells the world what an Indian entrepreneur can do: no mater whether he is making world-beating acoustic systems or plain Dal Bukhara!

22

The Farce of an Indian Election

It is indeed tragic the way we have begun conducting elections in our country: its almost as if there are no real issues that the people need to confront save for some retired and at times really ugly film-stars and this is very worrying. I was quite horrified to see Hema Malini repeat her Sholay line where as Basanti she was asking her audience in Jaipur to save her 'izzat' and vote the BJP into power. What do these politicians think of the people? And how can a party led by people like Vajpayee and Advani allow this nonsense to continue? Is there a dearth of reality in this party or for that matter the Samajwadi party, which had the faded villain Raza Murad campaigning for them? Do the politicians seriously believe that it is Sholay and not roads that they must remember whilst voting for someone. The manner in which these artists on hire have jumped onto the campaign bandwagon is equally disgusting. People like them for what they do best, which is act: not to inject self-reality by pretending to be either politicians or vote-pullers. And this is the enduring tragedy of Indian elections today. They have become a mela and in effect events more than serious business of establishing good governance. Closer home in Delhi, what the BJP is doing is equally shocking. Vijay Goel has helped launch stars on our streets that we may never have see or ever are likely to. This fetish for star power will hurt the politician even more than it will the electorate. I believe India has some serious issues such as corruption in the whole quagmire of governance; we have poor roads; no water and little power: it is this that must seize the attention of those who seek votes: by numbing the masses to some silly spectacle of star power is not only belying the people's mandate but equally their trust and this is something that must certainly prick the conscience of the Prime Minister and his Deputy. Look at Madhya Pradesh as a stark contrast to the drivel elsewhere. Jaitley has used spin doctoring effectively to create a people's movement where the real questions that are being asked are about real things. Digvijay Singh has performed miserably on the three planks of roads, power and water and Jaitley has focused on that and that alone. There is no tamasha about either mud-slinging or about deviating from the real issues that people will have to live with and live under.

I always thought the BJP was a party, which understood the issues of the people and steered clear of showmanship. But tragically they are just another party, which believes the issues of governance arise only from election to election, and not what happens in the interim! The BJP is today as rudderless as the Congress and I am not going to be surprised that Sheila Dikshit will romp home here in Delhi or for that matter, the son-of-the-soil Ashok Gehlot will trounce the chiffon maharani Vasundhara Scindia. And here it is not Scindia's fault. The party has catapulted her into a position of no win. She cannot compete for the Chief Ministership of a state where even today she is seen merely as a tourist! The party should have acted with greater gravitas but then I guess that is asking too much of ay political party in today's India. The fact that the BJP continues to use the services of Judeo (who is now also the subject of a story in TIME magazine) proves how thick-skinned our political leadership is. The fact that we have a seemingly wily person in the form of Ajit Jogi is no excuse to keep on using the services of a tainted and corrupt former Union Minister: this in itself is shocking! Indira Gandhi ruined the electoral process when she played havoc with issues and instead chose to divide the nation across communal lines: she destroyed an institution, which was the guarantor of good governance in any democracy. Today what the BJP is doing is something even worse. Not only is religion being sprinkled liberally, but what is more we are also seeing an injection of the farcical just so that they can grab a few more votes!

It is this despicable showing by the ruling party which should worry every Indian who will participate in these Assembly elections and in the General Elections next year. It is one thing to mock our soul but quite other to mock our intelligence and the more we allow these politicians to do this, the more we will see this country sink. But this is a choice that I guess each one of us has to make. And given our track record, we will fall prey to machinations which are at the best truly despicable!

23

The Business of Cricket

I went to see the finals of the TVS Cup in Calcutta earlier this week and was amazed by the emphasis on business and commerce that the cricket establishment is putting rather than on improving the game of Indians as it were which is why it is not surprising we were humbled in the way we were. Our country lacks good sports administrators in the true sense: except for Suresh Kalmadi and K P S Gill I cannot think of anyone else. Jagmohan Dalmiya is a first-rate businessman but one can hardly call him a cricket administrator and this is perhaps why the game is left to the mercy of people who use their powers at BCCI for reasons other than promoting cricket. Our selectors are a hopeless bunch of people: what more do you expect if you have a bumbling fool like Kirmani heading the Selectors for our country. No one at Eden Gardens could explain the inclusion of Salvi and the exclusion of Kaif in this match. Salvi was an unmitigated disaster for all to see. I am delighted that by the end of the match, when the team for the Australia tour was announced, Salvi had been dropped owing to some shoulder injury: the truth was no shoulder injury but pure incompetence! The fact that we have the whole cricket establishment in the hands of people who are not concerned about the advancement of the game but are instead of focusing on how thy can extract more money from sponsors will signal the death of cricket as we sued to know it. I saw people sitting in the Club House who were not even remotely connected with the game but were there as pure vultures and whose whole intention was to see how much money they could extract from people watching the game rather than let the true spirit of the game take over. The infusion of politics into the game is another early warning signal, which should tell us of the enormous subtle power that officialese in cricket wields.

Jagmohan Dalmiya has made Indian cricket an enterprise. Which is fine, but certainly not at the cost of quality cricket, which needs to be developed not just at the Shivaji Parks and the Calcutta Maidan, but also more importantly in schools and colleges which today lack funding options. The fact that the Board of Cricket Control in India is rich is not something to be proud of for the simple reason tat it is not intended to be a profit-making body: it is meat for the lateral development of the game and something that will help many more Indians make a relevant global statement. The fact that we today have an insipid cricket team, which can collapse once Tendulkar, and Dravid are out speaks very poorly of talent development, which is also one of the charters of this Board. The Board needs to expand its horizons and take off its blinkers if it means serious cricketing business. Commerce is not satisfying to anyone: be it a spectator or a sponsor if all we do is lose every match for silly reasons such as pathetic fielding or poor team selection.

I also believe that cricket in India and especially its controls are vested in a clique which refuses to admit people into it who are genuine proponents of this game: which is the enduring tragedy for the game. This game can no longer afford to be personality-driven ad ego-subsumed. It has to rise above all this and the sooner it does the better off we all will be. The development of the game must know no ego barriers or camps. It must recognise talent wherever it resides without worrying about parochialism since that alone has been the cause of our nation's downfall in almost every avenue. The fact that today the stakes in cricket are so high is also alarming because you are creating pressure points which have more to do with money ad less wit the actual sport!

Today our stadia need to be world-class; they need better safety requirements; they need better facilities for spectators: from food courts to better security and parking management but then all this is give the shirt shrift only because we are so myopic in our outlook towards the game and infact the Board only worries about its next re-election rather than the legacy of leaving behind a well-tended and robust game. If this trend is not arrested we will slowly lose the cricketing advantage as we did the hockey advantage.

24

Dinner with the Prince

It is not very often that one gets to dine with a real prince especially when matters of great importance have seized the world and we really need to wonder where we are headed. The dinner with Prince Charles was illuminating to say the least and I must confess that not only was he exceedingly charming but equally passionate about the causes he believes in: the dinner was mercifully small and unlike these large receptions which meant that we could have a decent and intelligent conversation rather than some unmindful social swirl. The dining-table conversation began with his rightful concerns regarding what is happening to food security around the world and thus the conversation focused largely on the havoc that genetically modified foods are causing. Prince Charles has championed the cause of a GM-free world for as long as I can remember and his belief is that the more we say from our roots, the more danger we will create for ourselves which in a manner of speaking is true. It is indeed sad that in our country we have a situation where there is absolutely no control over the issues that will impact future generation of Indians. If you see the agriculture policy that we have, you will observe there is a qualitative reduction in the food chain in India not to mention the gay abandon with which all norms of quality are being flouted; the excessive use of fertilizers and pesticides giving birth to generally unhealthy crops if you ca call them that. The Prince is therefore rightly worried that if we allow the world of modernity to completely sweep us off our feet, there will be very little left of our roots and that anchoring is critical to human development.

China whilst being a superior economic power is not the same as far as India's record of humanity and democracy is concerned: to that end the Prince whilst not commenting on a tricky issue such as this did not however hide his unabashed admiration for where India has travelled in the last ten to fifteen years. When asked if anything had changed since he last visited this country, he replied with unusual candour and great conviction that nothing must ever change so dramatically which ten upsets the image of the country you have. It is precisely this that I wish to address: for far too long we in India have adopted extremities of one kind or the other: either there is too much of the old-world that we wish to adopt and hanker after or there is too much of modernity that we seek in everything we do: the process of natural evolution that all civilizations must go through is being constantly ignored and that indeed is worrying. India has sacrificed the natural advantages that it is equipped with at the altar of a quick-fix modern solution to everything we encounter. This modernity decries all that we as a civilization have achieved over the past several hundred years and this will create a generation of Indians who will have no anchoring whatsoever. The MTVisation of India can work but only partially: it is sad that today when you talk of yoga you talk of Hollywood and not the ashrams that dot our country's landscape: for the same reason when you talk of spirituality there is an over-riding association with the Deepak Chopras of the world than with the real gurus who have not marketed themselves so efficiently and this is precisely the point that the Prince drove home: our roots and adherence to certain cultural indices is what will create an enduring national competitive advantage and this must be seen in the context of the essential difference between truly great nations and just rich nations per se. he also bemoaned the wanton destruction of cities and their landscape by people who gave the short shrift to design and appeal: to that end the Prince shared his pet project which is the creation of a model town in Dorset which will have all the ingredients of modern-day living without sacrificing eye-appeal or for that matter by destroying the basic character of the English countryside.

In the end, he came across as a ma who holds deep conviction unlike the politician or the bureaucrat: as a man who recognises that e must not waver from those convictions since they're being made with sincerity and have a purpose which is beneficial to humanity and as a man who realises that he has chosen a path which may not be treaded upon by all and sundry.

25

Is Transparency the Victim?

While very few people can ever doubt the integrity of Arun Shourie as a person, it is indeed troubling that Arun Shourie is compromising his image for no apparent reason in the telecom case as also in the larger process of disinvestments. Both of which do not augur well either for the Government he belongs to or for the ministries he is handling. Ad tat too in a Government which perhaps has the most transparent and efficient PMOs; a Government where the top leadership comprises people of the highest morality and integrity and a Government which has never been confrontational with any institution be it the judiciary or the Election Commission. It is tragic that today there is a constant war between the cellular operators and those providing WLL services and in this war Shourie is being portrayed the villain of the piece. Let us for a moment examine the facts of the telecom issue: when the Government opened out this sector, they invited people to bid for licenses: ad this Government then charged these people huge license fees: after some years, they then invited bids for yet another license in the mobility business at which time some of the existing operators bid and got licenses. At that time, while WLL was being bandied about, none of the WLL operators bid for the mobile license whereas if they wanted to provide mobile services, they could have. Today you have a situation in which both WLL and cellular operators are providing the same services but clearly only the cellular operators have paid a license fee whereas the others have not. Technically, the current WLL operators are providing an illegal service: it is akin to any one of us building a third or fourth floor on top of our existing homes illegally and then waiting for some Government legislation to legalize it. This is exactly the state that the world of telecom is in today. I have a basic and fundamental problem wit this approach. No Government can or must be seen to be even tacitly supporting anything illegal. The fact that the WLL operators have not been shut down is the first problem that Shourie has created. Then there is the issue of non-compliance of a judicial order. The TDSAT (equivalent to a High Court) has issued an order, which clearly states that what the WLL operators are doing is illegal and yet no action has been taken by Shourie. Instead what has happened is the Government has set up a Group of Ministers to examine this whole issue. This is illogical. Has the GoM been set up to legalize what is truly illegal in the present circumstances? There is much talk of a unified license but then why should something illegal continue just because you hope and believe you will establish a law that will legalise this illegality retrospectively. This bodes ill not only for the Government's image but makes the Government come across as bumbling fools and what's worse as a contempetener in the eyes of the law!

My worry is two-fold: not only is there a blatant disregard for the law that the Government itself has sown; there is also blatant disregard for its own policies so tomorrow if some private party blatantly blinks at the law, you would have already established a precedent where every illegality can continue till made legal! This is a comedy of errors and nothing more!

The Government must seem to act on this and not hide behind the coattails of its own GoM: you are clearly hoodwinking the consumer and also showing utter disrespect to the law: both of which are unforgivable.

My other concern is with this new found love for divesting IOC: this is yet another attempt at what I would call backdoor legalizing: the Supreme Court has clearly established a process for further divestment so why does Shourie or this Government now want to take on the Supreme Court and get rapped on the knuckles at is has in the past. This Government will destroy every plank of transparency that it has so well established in the five years only because someone in the Government has chosen to be a hero and be trigger-happy.

I am not aware of the politics behind all this but all I ca say is stop all this before it consumes everyone I this Government. Ad the time to act is now.

26

The Statesman of Our Times

I have, over the past few months, observed with admiration and delight, the evolution of Vajpayee as the statesman that India so desperately needed. Infact, I am no contender for any Rajya Sabha seat as some esteemed editors of this fragile land of ours are, so my words should not be misconstrued as prose in flattery. Its just that Vajpayee's track-record has been enviously wonderful as Prime Minister and this man has been able to inspire the faith ad belief of several people cutting across both the political and social divide. His stature is so enormous that it makes Sonia Gandhi look like a sulking school-girl who has just been asked to braid her air in pony-tails. Vajpayee's recent visit to China was symbolic of the respect that he commands not just in the region but on the global stage as well which is why when people talk of Musharraf being at Camp David with the Bushs, I am not too worried. I would much rather have a Prime Minister like Vajpayee who speaks his mind; is secular to the core and can keep factionalism at bay than have a rabid hawk as my leader.

Enough has also been written about L. K. Advani in our papers and he has unfairly been described the hawk of this Government. To give the man credit, there is no clearer thinker than him that this Government has and the two Aruns have miles to go before they can be as articulate or as astute as Advani. I believe the whole F 16 deal for the Pakistanis which the Americans had proposed was infact scuttled by Advani when he went to America and this is a tremendous achievement for India: even though not many have given Advani the credit e deserves.

When I look back at the India that both these gentlemen inherited from the corrupt goons that inhabited the Congress Party and then take a look at where we are today,

There is no question in my mind that we are far better off under the BJP than we ever were under the Congress except for the early 50s. Advani has demonstrated a high degree of value-based politics in everything he has done and I am sure Advani knows this better than I do, that he would never be as complete in his present role if he did not have a Vajpayee as his boss and his leader. Vajpayee's stirring qualities also include a high level of ambivalence when he chooses it. He can be vague yet delightfully quote-worthy which is why he is perhaps the only other statesman Prime Minister other than Nehru that we in India have ever had. All the other Prime Ministers have been dwarfs in comparison: dwarfs both in thought and belief not to mention deed!

Then there is the reality of decision-making that has happened in this Government. Arun Jaitley as the first Minister for Dis-investment and now Arun Shourie as the present minister have blazed a trail, which is enviable and popular: the recent Maruti IPO is a testimony to this. If you take a look at this Government's track record in law and order, never have we seen a calmer freer India. And the accusation of the BJP mixing politics and religion can hardly be made the murderers and revenge-seekers of the Congress who showed us their true colours during the 1984 riots!

I believe that India has also emerged a more stable economy notwithstanding the series of scams that were finally brought to light. Surely the Government can do a lot more but never have we seen a Government try as valiantly as this one and this is the true test of fine leadership. It has made efforts in creating path-breaking legislation which will at some stage in the future guarantee reservations for women in our parliament; it has set up fast-track courts and made the judiciary more and more accountable; it has stayed clear from politicizing the office of the President which is why ensconced in the Rashtrapati Bhavan today, we have a truly people's President who is creating history in his won way and contributing to the rapid change that India must be part of. This has truly been a Government that has empathized with the people. I have not heard murmurs of corruption emanating from any quarters of Government; the party's discipline has shown through with much aplomb as well: reflected in the fact that now a brilliant tactician in the form of Pramod Mahajan will be running the party while Naidu makes all the gaffes!

In sum, the statesman has done very well for India. And equally for himself. It has been a Government that we can truly be proud of. It has managed coalition politics in an almost text-book manner the seer magnetism of Vajpayee draws people of all hues to him or else how would you explain Jayalalithaa's second honeymoon with Vajpayee? Which is why without debating the future of either the RSS or the BJP, my vote for the next elections would go to Atal Bihari Vajpayee. The last (along with Advani) of the gentlemen in Indian politics.

27

Face to Face with God!

Apart from theatre and some really pretty women, I guess I have no other passion. I do not wish to become a Rajya Sabha member; I have no interest in becoming a hot-selling author who then becomes an activist with short hair or for that matter shouting for more causes than I can handle. Theatre is truly where my heart resides which is why when you meet your God, you are humbled. Not by the grandeur of his gift but by the spread of his art; by the innate wingspan of his talent and the intensity of purpose. I have always dreamt of meeting Al Pacino. Not because he was great in 'Godfather'. Not because he was sensational in 'Scent of a Woman' but because he has won two Tonys for theatrical excellence! Because he believes in theatre and is passionate enough to even make a play-reading come alive as if you were seeing movement of a rarefied kind. When I entered the Barrymore Theatre on the evening of 11 April 2003 I knew I would be coming into contact with heavenly powers. I had bought the ticket for Salome's opening night the day I landed in New York which was more than a fortnight before. It is not very often that you get to see Pacino in a play and its even rarer to see the man and talk to him which is exactly what happened. The play was brilliant. Al Pacino was simply stunning. He is unarguably the finest actor alive. I would put him any pegs higher than a Jack Nicholson or even a Marlon Brando.

The play commenced at 8 pm and was over by about 9.45 pm. Without an intermission. A continuos delight unfolding before awe-struck eyes. There were the usual gasps when Pacino first made an appearance. Awe changed very rapidly to innate admiration represented in a silence that I have rarely seen in New York what with Americans constantly chewing something or the other. But this was different. God was performing and his disciples just sat in amazement. And like some other Gods, this one did not disappoint, When the play ended I headed straight for backstage. Because when you see a great performance you head backstage. Again something that never happens in New York because people are either desperate to hail that reclusive cab or are rushing to make it on time for their dinner reservation. I was stopped only once: at the door to the back of the stage. I quickly spun a yarn of being Pacino's friend from India. Lies. But then who cares!

And then I came face to face with the man himself. It was almost as if some unmeasurable energy had been released and I began by saying, "Pacino you were tremendous ... I am from India and I have come all the way to New York only to see you perform." Lies again. But then who cares. He ushered me into the green room and then we began chatting as if we truly were long lost friends. I thought to myself, either this man is too bored or just needs someone to share his oxygen. But at the time, what was important was I was talking to the same man who did that amazing tango in Scent of a Womkan; the same man who won two Tonys; the same man who breathed life into Simone acting as a has-been film director.

We obviously started by talking about Salome: that is why he and I were there. "I don't believe in play-readings ... for me theatre is about being alive. It makes you breathe with some purpose. I have always consumed the smell of my audiences." Smell?, I asked, "Yes, the smell of the clothes they wear; the perfume; the drinks they've had in the foyer; the noise of the cough or the sucking of candy and then moments of silence. Because when they are silent, I know I've got them." I was quick to ask him if this was all the influence of his character in 'Scent of a Woman.' "Not at all. Theatre is something you never give up if you began life in it. Theatre has no de-addiction clinics. It is real. It is abut reality and not about re-takes."

Why did he return to theatre and too with Salome? "I am ere because I love New York and New York is what made me love theatre. We did stage this play privately in the Brooklyn area and were delighted with the response. Which is why we are doing it here. And we'll be at it for 59 performances and then I can go back to what I do for a living."

Has the craft in theatre in American suffered thanks to all these musicals? "I don't know. I really don't. I guess the craft has widened its spread. There are many who just want to laugh or just cry. They want entertainment for the mind. Serious theatre is entertainment for the soul. And the soul is what we all eventually want to protect."

I knew by the look on his face that my time was really running out. Gods have several duties to perform and it was opening night which would no doubt be followed by a small cast party (unlike India where cast parties are had after all the shows are over) so I got up with a question. What more do you have to achieve? You've done it all. "Ha. I wish that were true. I really do. Acting is like looking at a beautiful woman ... you want to see as many as you possibly can. The urge for acting is unending."

"What do you guys in India think about the war?" I had no answer. Anything I would say would border on the political and I didn't want to mar this special evening with an opinion. It was far too special.

As I exited from the theatre I looked up at the sky and it was almost in silent prayer. I had met my God. And more.

28

A Nation Short of Heroes

The recent anger of our countrymen against cricketers is more about being feel let down by the only heroes you have rather than being let down by a team that can actually win the World Cup. The truth of the matter is we in India have very few heroes left since there are no rewards for heroism. We reward brokers; political mavericks; corrupt corporate czars and scamsters. These are the people who earn our respect only because they first inspire fear us. Compared to that cricketers are so passive; they play a game and they hopefully are supposed to play it well so all the emotions we have, we shift towards tem in full measure and when they don't measure up we start attacking tem; we start burning their homes; we abuse them and pour vitriol all over them. But the truth is, we are abusing ourselves; cursing our own destinies as we shower insults on them. The saga of cricket in India is an enduring one and each one of us is responsible for turning mere sportsmen into Gods. We have done that only because it suited us. Not suited the cricketers. We have done it out of our own selfishness; we have done it to own tem and in a sense bask on that borrowed glory. I was shocked to hear that in Kolkata some fans had taken out a mock funeral procession of the cricketers. Every Kolkatan is a hypocrite only when he or se chooses to be. That is the same city which breeds Jagmohan Dalmiya who is essence is the cancer of Indian cricket. Who has transformed the game of bat and ball into the game of politics and sleaze!

The malaise of Indian cricket is its overriding concerns about commerce. Our cricketers earn more money by shooting for television commercials and print advertisements than by playing cricket. So you would do the next logical thing and blame them for shooting; blame them for spending time in the studio; blame them for not concentrating on their game but in reality blame yourself. Companies use cricketers because people like you and me worship them. Because people like you and me get carried away with their persona. We begin to believe they will be just as good with a motorcycle as they are tackling a googly so we go ahead and lose our rationality when it comes to anything they do. Much like the manner in which we treat our cine stars. So if anyone is to be blamed it is us. And yes, the people who administer the game of cricket. They need to recognise that cricket in India has achieved religious proportions. People are mesmerized beyond repair and this is something that they need to be cognizant of: but the tragedy is that greed and avarice knows no bounds in the people who control the management of cricket. For them it is about unbridled power; it is about control and not about progressing the game; it is about sucking up to the stars that exist in the team and not about looking for and grooming new talent. Which is why a country of more than a billion people can barely put together a half-decent cricket team!

The real issue is not about how good or bad our cricketers are. The issue is how a nation can raise stars to dizzy eights before bringing them down with equal ease. The issue is not about our cricketers letting us down; it is about how we have allowed them to impact our lives so very much that we wish to stop buying products they endorse! We have allowed cricket to invade our senses. We may never go to war with Pakistan yet every cricket match played against Pakistan is about a proxy war. I am convinced that each Indian will forgive India for their performance thus far if we manage to score a victory against Pakistan: never mind if this Pakistani team is the weakest amongst the lot we have played in the past! Never mind if do not win the world cup but that one victory against Pakistan will warm the cockles of our collective hearts. That's the opium for the Indian masses today and we feel disgusted whenever we don't win.

Our cricketers are just ordinary human beings with perhaps an extraordinary flair for cricket. That is about it. But we have converted them to demi-gods and it is only our collective disdain when our Gods let us down.

Isn't that ironic? In a country where there is a God at every street corner we have to wait for a team of eleven to expose our vulnerability? To show how crestfallen we are? To prove to the world how fanatically we live our dreams through some odd willow-wielders? But then I guess that is the paradox that India is!

I hope India wins the World Cup. We can't have a crestfallen nation just because we didn't win the game of bat and ball!

29

The Wheels of Justice

I was delighted by the verdict of the Delhi High Court on the Uphaar tragedy. For several reasons. Over the last five or six years I have relentlessly pursued this cause even though I wasn't living in Delhi when this tragedy occurred; for the fact that no matter how much ruse and guise and manipulation that the Ansals must have used, they couldn't get away; for the fact that people whose lives have been destroyed can atleast have the satisfaction of seeing those who made this so, be punished even if only financially. I would have been happier if the people accused were put behind bars never to surface again. This is the kind of punishment that will set an example. In our country the rich and the powerful can almost always get away and re-start their lives in a supplicant society tat is only too willing to embrace them once they believe they are not criminals any longer. But for a moment consider the response that the Ansals had to the judgement. This was even more appalling and I am surprised that no newspaper has yet commented on this. Sushil Ansal was quoted as saying that while we have been punished, so has the Delhi Vidyut Board and the Delhi Police as if suggesting they were not the guilty party alone. Is the transference of guilt a virtue Ansal or are you trying to be deflective in a real crass manner? I wonder which of these is your attempt to re-instate your honour if you have any? In any event, I hope there will be no passing the buck by the Government where the Government will now expect the private power companies to pay the for the sins of the erstwhile DVB. That too, should be objected to vehemently by the private power companies. The DVB should pay their share and they alone should pay it. They should not get the private sector to pay for what was clearly their fault!

Go any of the buildings that the Ansals own or run in Delhi and each one of them is a virtual fire hazard. If you go the Ambaddep Building, there is also a warning pasted outside the elevator saying that you are taking the elevator at your own risk. My friend C. K. Birla has his office in an Ansal building and it is a virtual death-trap but then this is what these people do. They allow these buildings to become virtual death-traps and then calmly shift the blame to other parties. My recommendation on this would be to punish these people and make examples out of them. Punish them so hard that no one ever thinks of breaking or worse still tweaking the law. Because until you don't, we will continue to have many more Uphaars.

Mukul Mudgal's judgement is superb. It is courageous and shows the whole judiciary in tremendous light. Mukul has shown the judiciary to be humane and citizen-centric. It has also told the world that we are after all a democracy where the law will ultimately get you no matter how powerful or wealthy you may be. My advise to the Ansals would be to now issue a public apology; erect an Uphaar Memorial Garden and share the grief of those families that lost their beloved thanks to their negligence. That would be true commitment to people who you make money from.

The judgement has also set another benchmark in the compensation domain that people can expect from those who inflict fatal and grave damage to the lives of the average citizen, To that end, Mukul has set a standard that can only improve with the passage of time when India's history of jurisprudence will be written. My only request to those who run India's judiciary is please hurry things up when it comes to issues such as these. The trauma that the families go through can never be imagined or understood by those who haven't gone through it. It is a time that makes one feel miserably helpless: a time when you lose faith not just in humanity but at a pinch, even in God. The agony of fighting so hard for so long just after such anguish is something we can well avoid by taking steps that will help justice arrive firmer and quicker.

The Uphaar tragedy will be remembered for the insensitivity of those who run public facilities; it will be remembered for their lack of generosity and for their manipulative streak; it will also be remembered for the crassness in which one family tried to do everything in its power to hide from accountability right from the time members of that family were evading arrest and so on.

But thankfully it will also be remembered for the justice that was finally meted out to the families that had everything to lose. That alone renews my hope and faith in this great country of ours!